Samuel French Acting Edition

The Keen Collection
One-Acts by Contemporary Playwrights
Volume 2

Going Left
by Kristoffer Diaz

Syd Arthur
by Kenny Finkle

Why Aren't You Dead Already
by Halley Feiffer

SAMUELFRENCH.COM   SAMUELFRENCH.CO.UK

Going Left Copyright © 2015 by Kristoffer Diaz
Syd Arthur Copyright © 2015 by Kenny Finkle
Why Aren't You Dead Already Copyright © 2015 by Halley Feiffer
All Rights Reserved

THE KEEN COLLECTION: VOLUME 2 is fully protected under the copyright laws of the United States of America, the British Commonwealth, including Canada, and all member countries of the Berne Convention for the Protection of Literary and Artistic Works, the Universal Copyright Convention, and/or the World Trade Organization conforming to the Agreement on Trade Related Aspects of Intellectual Property Rights. All rights, including professional and amateur stage productions, recitation, lecturing, public reading, motion picture, radio broadcasting, television and the rights of translation into foreign languages are strictly reserved.

ISBN 978-0-573-70433-8

www.SamuelFrench.com
www.SamuelFrench.co.uk

FOR PRODUCTION ENQUIRIES

UNITED STATES AND CANADA
Info@SamuelFrench.com
1-866-598-8449

UNITED KINGDOM AND EUROPE
Plays@SamuelFrench.co.uk
020-7255-4302

Each title is subject to availability from Samuel French, depending upon country of performance. Please be aware that *THE KEEN COLLECTION: VOLUME 2* may not be licensed by Samuel French in your territory. Professional and amateur producers should contact the nearest Samuel French office or licensing partner to verify availability.

CAUTION: Professional and amateur producers are hereby warned that *THE KEEN COLLECTION: VOLUME 2* is subject to a licensing fee. Publication of this play(s) does not imply availability for performance. Both amateurs and professionals considering a production are strongly advised to apply to Samuel French before starting rehearsals, advertising, or booking a theater. A licensing fee must be paid whether the title(s) is presented for charity or gain and whether or not admission is charged. Professional/Stock licensing fees are quoted upon application to Samuel French.

No one shall make any changes in this title(s) for the purpose of production. No part of this book may be reproduced, stored in a retrieval system, or transmitted in any form, by any means, now known or yet to be invented, including mechanical, electronic, photocopying, recording, videotaping, or otherwise, without the prior written permission of the publisher. No one shall upload this title(s), or part of this title(s), to any social media websites.

For all enquiries regarding motion picture, television, and other media rights, please contact Samuel French.

MUSIC USE NOTE

Licensees are solely responsible for obtaining formal written permission from copyright owners to use copyrighted music in the performance of this play and are strongly cautioned to do so. If no such permission is obtained by the licensee, then the licensee must use only original music that the licensee owns and controls. Licensees are solely responsible and liable for all music clearances and shall indemnify the copyright owners of the play(s) and their licensing agent, Samuel French, against any costs, expenses, losses and liabilities arising from the use of music by licensees. Please contact the appropriate music licensing authority in your territory for the rights to any incidental music.

IMPORTANT BILLING AND CREDIT REQUIREMENTS

If you have obtained performance rights to this title, please refer to your licensing agreement for important billing and credit requirements.

TABLE OF CONTENTS

Foreword 7
Keen Teens Angels...................................... 8
Going Left... 9
Syd Arthur 31
Why Aren't You Dead Already 57

FOREWORD

It's my pleasure to introduce you to the collected works from the eighth season of Keen Company's Keen Teens – a season which I think has been our bravest one yet. Since I began working with this program as a director in the first season, I have been amazed by how combining professional playwrights with the energy of young people has resulted in powerful new work. Throughout the spring of 2014, I watched both new and returning Keen Teens use their work on these plays not only as an opportunity to strengthen their work as actors, but also as an opportunity to engage deeply and honestly with the world around them.

Thornton Wilder called the theater "the most immediate way in which a human being can share with another the sense of what it is to be a human being." And there's so much more to being a young human being in America today than who is and isn't popular at their high school, although that's the lens through which we consistently see young people represented in entertainment. In our 2014 Keen Teens plays, you'll see how our young people explored contemporary issues in meaningful, complex ways.

Set in the world of high school basketball, *Going Left* by Kristoffer Diaz explores the excitement and confusion of the search for young love. In our production, the fact that both point guards were men went as unremarked upon onstage as it was unremarkable offstage. Based on a real-life event, Halley Feiffer's *Why Aren't You Dead Already* offers a harrowing, emotional look at the consequences of cyberbullying. In Kenny Finkle's *Syd Arthur*, young people grapple with the kind of loss that's much deeper than losing a prom queen competition or a football game.

The experience of working on these plays had a powerful effect on all of us. From the first read-through, it was clear that these young people were being given the chance to speak out in ways that were rare for them. Gasps commingled with raucous laughter. Teens looked to one another, as if to affirm that, yes, we were going there. Most of all, they wanted to talk. I hope in reading these plays you'll experience the joy that went into creating them and the unmatchable thrill that comes from young people raising their voices.

Thank you to all our wonderful cast members and their families for being part of this incredible journey. Keen Company's audiences experienced the world premieres of these magnificent plays, but through our partnership with Samuel French, this work will live on for generations. Enjoy.

– *Mark Armstrong*
Director of New Work
Keen Company

KEEN TEENS ANGELS

Cathy and Robert Altholz, Harrison and Leslie Bains, Amy and Brad Ball, Jeff and Tina Bolton, Bill and Casey Bradford, Kathleen Chalfant, Buena Chilstrom, Brian d'Arcy James and Jennifer Prescott, Kate and Steve Davis, Lucy and Nat Day, Patricia Follert, Ray and Cathy Garea, Timothy Grandia, Albert R. and Molly Gurney, Jennifer Jahn, Missy and Ed Kelly, David and Kate Kies, Anki Leeds, Marsha Mason, Donna and Jack McCoy, Erik Piecuch, Carol Quint, Charles Rubinger (in memory of Gail Rubinger), Vincent Smith and Alice Silkworth, Mike Emmerman and Pat Stockhausen, Barry Waldorf and Stanley Gotlin, Alban Wilson, Ernest and Judith Wong

Going Left

Kristoffer Diaz

GOING LEFT was first presented by Keen Company (Jonathan Silverstein, Artistic Director; Mark Armstrong, Director of New Work) and Samuel French, Inc. as part of the 2014 Keen Teens Festival of New Work. The performance was directed by Daisy Walker, with sets by Colin McGurk, costumes by Ricola Wille, lights by Jeffrey Toombs, and original music and sound design by M. Florian Staab. The Production Stage Manager was Ryan Parow. The cast was as follows:

DREXLER/HORNACEK . . . . Zac Ball
MR. D/BOWIE/MULLIN . . . . Junior Duplessis
MALONE/RICHMOND . . . . Marcus Edward
PETRO . . . . .Ralphie Irizzary
COLEMAN/OAKLEY . . . . Nicholas Johnson
STOCKTON . . . . Michael Alexander Lopez
MRS. Q . . . . Heavenly Martinez
HARDAWAY'S MOM . . . . Kimberly McBride
BIRD . . . . Bahsil Moody
HARDAWAY . . . . Skyler Scott
MORRIS/WAITER . . . . Woodensky Thomas

CHARACTERS

DREXLER
HORNACEK
MR. D
BOWIE
MULLIN
MALONE
RICHMOND
PETRO
COLEMAN
OAKLEY
STOCKTON
MRS. Q
HATHAWAY'S MOM
BIRD
HARDAWAY
MORRIS
WAITER

SETTING

The Land of High School Basketball.

TIME

Present Day.

1.

HARDAWAY. Hey.
STOCKTON. Hi.
HARDAWAY. Hey.
STOCKTON. Hi.
HARDAWAY. I know you.
STOCKTON. No.
HARDAWAY. I do.
STOCKTON. No.
HARDAWAY. You play basketball, right?
STOCKTON. No.
HARDAWAY. You don't?
STOCKTON. I mean, yeah, I do.
HARDAWAY. I know.
STOCKTON. How?
HARDAWAY. I've seen you.
STOCKTON. No.
HARDAWAY. I have, really.
STOCKTON. Why?
HARDAWAY. Why have I seen you?
STOCKTON. Yeah. Why have you seen me?
HARDAWAY. I play too.
STOCKTON. Have we played?
HARDAWAY. I like the way you play.
STOCKTON. No.
HARDAWAY. I do!
STOCKTON. Stop.
HARDAWAY. You go left good.
STOCKTON. I'm lefty.

HARDAWAY. That explains it.

STOCKTON. Can you go left good?

HARDAWAY. I'm righty.

STOCKTON. Some righties can still go left.

HARDAWAY. Do you want to go out some time?

STOCKTON. No.

HARDAWAY. You don't?

STOCKTON. Stop.

HARDAWAY. You want me to stop asking you out? Or asking you questions in general?

STOCKTON. You're messing with me.

HARDAWAY. No.

STOCKTON. Come on.

HARDAWAY. No, I'm not messing with you.

STOCKTON. You want to go out with me?

HARDAWAY. I know people don't say "oh you want to go out with me some time" really in real life anymore, but I don't know, I kind of want to go out with you.

STOCKTON. Kind of.

HARDAWAY. Really.

STOCKTON. You really kind of want to go out with me?

HARDAWAY. I really really want to go out with you.

STOCKTON. No. Stop.

HARDAWAY. Stop wanting to go out with you?

STOCKTON. That's not what I mean.

HARDAWAY. I know.

STOCKTON. So wait.

HARDAWAY. Waiting.

STOCKTON. You saw me play?

HARDAWAY. A couple of times, yeah.

STOCKTON. And you want to go out with me because you saw me play?

HARDAWAY. I like the way you go left.

2.

PETRO. Wait.

BIRD. Hold on.

MALONE. What?

BIRD. Who?

MALONE. He saw you play?

PETRO. Uh uh.

BIRD. I don't like this.

STOCKTON. I thought you guys were my friends.

PETRO. We're your friends.

MALONE. This is not going to be that.

STOCKTON. Not going to be what?

BIRD. Not going to be one of those things where you think we're jealous of you.

STOCKTON. I didn't say you were jealous.

BIRD. This is not going to be one of those things.

PETRO. And it's not going to be one of those things where you're in love, and we're preventing you from being in love just cause we don't think he's right for you, and we don't really know him, and if we just got to know him, we'd think he's so good and we'd understand that he's so good for you – this is not that, and this is not going to be that.

STOCKTON. I'm not in love.

MALONE. We know you're not in love.

STOCKTON. I didn't say I was in love.

BIRD. We know you.

PETRO. We know how you get.

STOCKTON. How do I get?

PETRO. You know how you get.

STOCKTON. I don't get like anything.

FLASHBACK 1.

(*A sign that reads: THIS IS HOW YOU GET.*)

STOCKTON. I don't know, it just feels different, you know? He's not the nicest guy maybe, not when you first meet him, and I don't know, my friends think he's kind of maybe boring. And they tell me I'm better than him, and that's sweet, right, but they don't really know him, and if they just got to know him, they'd know he's good and they'd understand that he's good for me.

MR. D. I'm your math teacher.

FLASHBACK 2.

BIRD. He's not always like this.

PETRO. He just gets lost sometimes.

MALONE. We're his friends. We support him, but.

PETRO. It's the new guy.

MALONE. It's definitely the new guy.

BIRD. We don't like him.

PETRO. And believe me, we are not that kind of friend who just doesn't like anyone.

MALONE. He's just not okay.

PETRO. He's not good.

BIRD. And we don't want to get to know him. Does that make us bad people?

WAITER. I don't even know who you all are. This is a diner. Do you want to order something?

BIRD. Cheese fries?

MALONE. Yeah, cheese fries are good.

FLASHBACK 3.

STOCKTON. My friends don't understand, and I expect them to understand, they're my teammates, you know? But every time I go out with someone, every time someone's interested even, my teammates aren't there for me. And I expect them to be there, because on the court they're there, right? And if I can't count on them to be there for me when I'm starting to get serious about someone, how can I count on them to be there for me on the court?

BOWIE. Are we getting serious?

STOCKTON. That's not what I'm saying.

BOWIE. This is our first date.

STOCKTON. So you think I'm talking too much?

BOWIE. I gotta go.

(Back to the scene.)

STOCKTON. Okay, I know how I get. But I'm not getting like anything right now.

BIRD. Where did you say you two met?

STOCKTON. I don't know, we were out, and we met. Why does that matter?

PETRO. And why did he come over and talk to you?

STOCKTON. I don't know. He wanted to ask me out.

MALONE. Why did he want to ask you out?

STOCKTON. I don't know. He liked me?

MALONE. How did he know he liked you?

STOCKTON. I thought you guys were my friends.

BIRD. We are. This isn't that. Stop.

PETRO. He just liked you because he thought you were cute?

STOCKTON. What? I can't be cute?

MALONE. You're very cute.

STOCKTON. Thanks.

MALONE. Is that why he said he liked you?

STOCKTON. He said he liked the way I went left.

PETRO. Oh. Stop.

BIRD. You gotta stop right now.

STOCKTON. What? Why?

BIRD. He liked the way you went left?

MALONE. Were you driving a race car?

STOCKTON. He meant playing basketball.

PETRO. We know he meant playing basketball.

MALONE. Were you playing basketball?

HARDAWAY. When?

BIRD. What do you mean, when? Come on.

PETRO. Were you playing basketball when you met him?

STOCKTON. No.

PETRO. He's a big high school basketball fan then?

STOCKTON. He plays.

MALONE. For who?

STOCKTON. What difference does that make?

BIRD. Who does he play for?

STOCKTON. This is ridiculous. I'm not talking to you guys anymore.

PETRO. Who does he play for? And when do we play them?

STOCKTON. We play them next week.

3.

HARDAWAY. No. Stop.

MORRIS. You are unbelievable.

DREXLER. I can't believe your dedication.

HARDAWAY. Dedication?

COLEMAN. Week before we play them.

DREXLER. And you got a date.

HARDAWAY. Dedication?

MORRIS. I wouldn't even think of that. A date? Who thinks of a date?

HARDAWAY. Are you making fun of me?

DREXLER. We probably will make fun of you, but right now, I'm kind of in awe.

MORRIS. We play them next week. You asked their point guard out this week.

COLEMAN. It's genius, I admit.

HARDAWAY. Oh no. Stop. Wait.

COLEMAN. We're not going to tell anybody.

DREXLER. Who would we tell?

MORRIS. Why would we tell anybody?

HARDAWAY. Tell anybody what?

DREXLER. You're committed. We respect that.

COLEMAN. It's like I don't think I'm pulling my weight. Feel like I should get in the gym or something. Maybe shoot an extra five hundred free throws.

DREXLER. You do need to shoot more free throws.

HARDAWAY. Wait. What are you talking about?

MORRIS. You're an inspiration!

HARDAWAY. For getting a date?

DREXLER. For getting a date with their point guard.

MORRIS. That makes me an inspiration?

COLEMAN. A week before we play them.

DREXLER. Yeah. That makes you an inspiration.

COLEMAN. We're in their heads already, you know.

HARDAWAY. I'm not trying to get in anybody's head.

MORRIS. Stop. Who are you trying to lie to?

HARDAWAY. I'm not lying to anybody.

DREXLER. You're trying to get in their heads.

COLEMAN. You're always trying to get in someone's head.

MORRIS. You're probably trying to get into my head right now. I'm onto you.

HARDAWAY. What? I can't actually want to ask somebody out?

MORRIS. No.

DREXLER. You? You in particular? No, you can't.

COLEMAN. You definitely can't. Not without wanting something else.

HARDAWAY. Come on.

COLEMAN. You always want something else.

MORRIS. You probably want something from me right now. I'm still onto you.

HARDAWAY. I don't always want something else.

DREXLER. Yeah. Yeah you do.

COLEMAN. You're always looking for an edge.

HARDAWAY. An edge?

DREXLER. Yeah. An edge. Stop pretending you don't know what we're talking about.

MORRIS. You're probably just trying to get an edge on us right now!

HARDAWAY. I'm not always looking for an edge.

FLASHBACK 4.

(*A sign that reads: YOU'RE ALWAYS LOOKING FOR AN EDGE.*)

MRS. Q. Is this an apple?

HARDAWAY. I know it's a cliche, but great teachers deserve an apple, right?

MRS. Q. And is this a Tupperware full of brownies?

HARDAWAY. I just made some extra brownies. Thought you might like some.

MRS. Q. Does this have anything to do with your term paper that I'm about grade?

HARDAWAY. Oh, you're about to grade my term paper? I had no idea.

FLASHBACK 5.

MORRIS. Okay, we're all done cleaning the garage.

HARDAWAY'S MOM. Wait. You guys were cleaning the garage?

DREXLER. Yeah, we know. But he bought us all this pizza.

HARDAWAY'S MOM. Cleaning the garage was his chore to do.

COLEMAN. Yeah, we know. But we love pizza.

DREXLER. We like really love pizza.

HARDAWAY'S MOM. How is he ever going to take care of his own responsibilities?

MORRIS. I mean, he still took care of it.

DREXLER. He just got us to take care of it.

COLEMAN. And we got pizza! So, you know, everybody wins.

FLASHBACK 6.

HARDAWAY. Pancakes! Pancakes for everyone!

MULLIN. Whoa, pancakes!

OAKLEY. We love pancakes!

HARDAWAY. No way! Come have some! We've got plenty!

RICHMOND. I don't know, guys. We've got a game in an hour. Pancakes could really weigh us down.

HARDAWAY. These are super delicious. And they've got chocolate chips.

OAKLEY. Chocolate chips!

HORNACEK. Maybe we can just try one.

HARDAWAY. That's a great idea. Just try one!

RICHMOND. It's a really big game, guys.

HARDAWAY. No way. You guys have a game today? Me too.

HORNACEK. You do? Who are you playing?

HARDAWAY. Totally doesn't matter! Go eat all the pancakes you want!

MULLIN. We will! Are you coming too?

HARDAWAY. I'll be right in. I swear I will! Eat lots of pancakes!

(Back to the scene.)

COLEMAN. Maybe you just like to give people food.

HARDAWAY. So maybe I have accidentally take advantage of people one or twice in my life.

MORRIS. Accidentally?

COLEMAN. Once or twice?

DREXLER. You are constantly giving people stuff to get them on your side.

MORRIS. And maybe you're not going on this date just to get the opposing team's point guard on your side a week before we play them.

HARDAWAY. I'm not.

MORRIS. Maybe you're not.

DREXLER. But probably you are.

COLEMAN. And we are totally fine with that.

HARDAWAY. No way. This is not that.

MORRIS. It's not?

HARDAWAY. It's not.

DREXLER. Then what is it?

HARDAWAY. I don't know. I like him.

MORRIS. You like him.

COLEMAN. Do you even know him?

HARDAWAY. Not really. No.

DREXLER. And you like him. Why do you like him?

HARDAWAY. I don't know. I like the way he goes left.

COLEMAN. What does that even mean?

MORRIS. It means he's got a good dribble to the left side.
COLEMAN. I know that's what it means.
HARDAWAY. Not everyone can do go left all that well.
DREXLER. He's lefty. He's supposed to be able to go left.
HARDAWAY. I know.
MORRIS. You're not making a very good argument. But don't worry. You don't have to convince us.
COLEMAN. And we're not going to tell anyone.
DREXLER. We're just impressed.
COLEMAN. I'm going to go shoot free throws.
DREXLER. Yeah, you need to shoot more free throws.
HARDAWAY. Guys. This isn't about getting an edge.
MORRIS. Hey, if it helps us win, call it anything you want.

4.

MALONE. Hey.

MORRIS. Hey.

PETRO. Hey.

DREXLER. Hey.

BIRD. Hey.

COLEMAN. Oh hi. How's it going, fellas?

MALONE. We're going to win.

MORRIS. Oh. Okay.

PETRO. We're going to beat you.

DREXLER. You're probably not going to beat us.

BIRD. We're better than you.

COLEMAN. You guys are really sophisticated trash talkers.

DREXLER. But you're not going to win.

MALONE. And we know what you're up to.

PETRO. We know what you're always up to.

BIRD. What your point guard is up to.

MALONE. What your point guard is always up to.

MORRIS. Whose point guard? Our point guard? No. Our point guard's never up to anything.

COLEMAN. Well, that's not true.

DREXLER. Yeah. He's usually up to something.

MORRIS. Okay, fine. But so what if he is?

MALONE. He is.

MORRIS. Okay, fine. But so what if he is?

BIRD. So nothing.

PETRO. Doesn't matter.

BIRD. That's our point.

MALONE. We're going to beat you anyway.

DREXLER. Okay, good. You're not. But it's good you think you are.

BIRD. And if any broken hearts come out of this thing...

MORRIS. Whoa!

COLEMAN. Whoa!

DREXLER. Whoa! Who said anything about broken hearts?

PETRO. We know how your point guard does things.

BIRD. And he's not in our heads.

COLEMAN. Sounds like he's in your heads.

BIRD. He's not in our heads.

MALONE. We just don't want anybody to get hurt.

DREXLER. Is that a threat?

PETRO. No. We just said we don't want anybody to get hurt. How could that be a threat?

DREXLER. Oh. Right. That's good. We don't want anyone to get hurt either.

MALONE. We just want to win.

PETRO. And we're going to.

MORRIS. You're not going to.

BIRD. Oh, we're going to.

DREXLER. No. You're not going to.

MALONE. Oh yeah we are.

COLEMAN. You might. What? It's possible you might. And if you do, we'll shake your hand and say good game.

BIRD. See, now that's sophisticated trash talk.

COLEMAN. It's not trash talk.

MORRIS. Maybe he's just getting in your head.

COLEMAN. I'm not.

MORRIS. Maybe he is.

MALONE. That's fine. It doesn't work. From you or from your point guard.

PETRO. We're going to win.

BIRD. We are definitely going to win.

DREXLER. We'll see.

BIRD. Yeah. We will.

MORRIS. Well then. Let's play some basketball.

5.

STOCKTON. Hey.

HARDAWAY. Hey.

STOCKTON. Hi.

HARDAWAY. Hi.

STOCKTON. Game's today.

HARDAWAY. Yup.

STOCKTON. Hope you play well.

HARDAWAY. Me too. Hope you play well, I mean.

STOCKTON. No, I know.

HARDAWAY. Yeah, I know you know.

STOCKTON. But not too well.

HARDAWAY. Ha. I know.

STOCKTON. Not well enough to beat us.

HARDAWAY. No, of course.

STOCKTON. I mean, I want you to play really well.

HARDAWAY. No, I know. I want you to play really well too.

STOCKTON. I just want to play better. Than you.

HARDAWAY. Yeah. Me too.

STOCKTON. Or no, wait. I want my team to play better than your team.

HARDAWAY. Yeah, totally. You can play better than me. I just want my team to win.

STOCKTON. Right. I want my team to win too.

HARDAWAY. Totally.

STOCKTON. But you can play better.

HARDAWAY. Thanks. I want you to play better than me too.

STOCKTON. Thanks.

HARDAWAY. Thanks.

STOCKTON. Thanks.

HARDAWAY. It's not really possible that we can both play better and both of our teams can win.

STOCKTON. Right.

HARDAWAY. Yep.

STOCKTON. Well.

HARDAWAY. Yeah.

STOCKTON. That's a problem.

HARDAWAY. Yep. Hey, listen.

STOCKTON. Okay.

HARDAWAY. We should talk.

STOCKTON. Okay.

HARDAWAY. I'm not trying to get an edge.

STOCKTON. Okay. What?

HARDAWAY. Huh?

STOCKTON. Not trying to get an edge? What edge?

HARDAWAY. You know, an edge.

STOCKTON. Oh, an edge. No, still don't know what you mean.

HARDAWAY. By going on a date.

STOCKTON. Oh. No, still don't know what you mean.

HARDAWAY. Well, it doesn't matter. But I'm not going on a date just to get an edge.

STOCKTON. Oh. I hadn't thought you were.

HARDAWAY. Oh.

STOCKTON. I thought you asked me out because you like me.

HARDAWAY. I did.

STOCKTON. You did?

HARDAWAY. I do. Like you.

STOCKTON. Oh.

HARDAWAY. Yeah.

STOCKTON. Oh good. And I'm not in love with you.

HARDAWAY. Whoa.

STOCKTON. No, I mean, if you think I am.

HARDAWAY. I didn't think you were.

STOCKTON. No, good.

HARDAWAY. But I mean, if you don't want to go out with me.

STOCKTON. No, I do!

HARDAWAY. But if you don't like me –

STOCKTON. No, I do!

HARDAWAY. You do?

STOCKTON. I do.

HARDAWAY. I thought you just said –

STOCKTON. No, I said I don't love you. In case you thought I did.

HARDAWAY. Oh. I didn't.

STOCKTON. Oh. Good.

HARDAWAY. Good.

STOCKTON. Okay.

HARDAWAY. Yup.

STOCKTON. Cool.

HARDAWAY. Yeah.

STOCKTON. Cool.

HARDAWAY. Got it.

STOCKTON. Yup.

MALONE. Hey! Game time!

MULLIN. Let's go!

DREXLER. Stop messing around!

HARDAWAY. Oh. We should go.

PETRO. Get your mind in the game!

COLEMAN. It's a big game!

BIRD. I hope you're not wasting your time on what I think you're wasting your time on.

STOCKTON. Am I wasting my time?

HARDAWAY. I don't think you are.

STOCKTON. I don't think I am either.

HARDAWAY. Okay.

OAKLEY. Let's go, let's go!

HARDAWAY. Can we still go out after the game?

PETRO. Game time!

STOCKTON. Yeah. I'd like that.

(All the other players call **STOCKTON** *and* **HARDAWAY**, *leading them away from each other.)*

HARDAWAY. Hey.

STOCKTON. Hey.

HARDAWAY. Have a really good game.

STOCKTON. I will. You too.

HARDAWAY. I will.

STOCKTON. Hope so.

(BLACKOUT. END OF PLAY.)

Syd Arthur

Kenny Finkle

with original songs by finkle

SYD ARTHUR was first presented by Keen Company (Jonathan Silverstein, Artistic Director; Mark Armstrong, Director of New Work) and Samuel French, Inc. as part of the 2014 Keen Teens Festival of New Work. The performance was directed by Jesse Geiger, with sets by Colin McGurk, costumes by Ricola Wille, lights by Jeffrey Toombs, and original music and sound design by M. Florian Staab. The Production Stage Manager was Ryan Parow. The cast was as follows:

MARTIN..Misael Azcona
MAX/JIMMY .... Christian Benenati
JAN .... Dara Pohl Feldman
LOUISE/LOU THE SECURTY GUARD.................... Zoe Marcel
ELIOT THE BOSS MAN/BARRY...................... Bahsil Moody
JONI ....Maya Pagan
GO.. Berk Pearlstein
MANUFACTURED POP STAR/PATRIZIA ....Destinee Eliana Perez
CARY THE CRAZY CREW GUY/MAC .... Fallon Sullivan
SYD .... Karla Ynfante

CHARACTERS

DEADPAN CHORUS (1-5 PEOPLE) – Speak in a deadpan, our friends.

SYD – Short for Sydney, 16, punkish, smart, big, interested.

GO – 19. Syd's only friend, been kind of lost for awhile.

JAN – Syd's Mom.

MARTIN – Syd's Dad.

CARY THE CRAZY CREW GUY – Name says it all.

MANUFACTURED POP STAR – Use your imagination.

LOU THE SECURITY GUARD – Has a blood sugar problem.

ELIOT THE BOSSMAN – Dillweed.

LOUISE – Hard to tell her age. really nice until threatened.

MAC – Older, big-hearted belly laugh kind of guy.

BARRY – Smart, in love with Joni, which makes him weak.

JONI – She is old beyond reason. kind of like a spiritual guru.

JIMMY – 20s. (mostly) silent heart-throb.

PATRIZIA – 50s. Italian Yoga Instructor.

MAX – 19. Syd's brother.

TIME

Now.

PLACE

A town somewhere in the middle of the desert

WORLD

optimistic, at times ironic, questioning, serious, scary, passionate, violent, irreverent, windy, moody.

NOTE

The Deadpan Chorus can be divided, broken up as the production demands. In the original production the director made choices about which lines were for ALL and which could be individual based on what the story needed.

(Light up on an empty stage. The **DEADPAN CHORUS** *enter. They stand in silence a moment. Then, begin.)*

DEADPAN CHORUS. This is the story of Sydney A Arthur
And her Quest for Meaning.
We're the Deadpan Chorus.
We're gonna start here.

(The **DEADPAN CHORUS** *seems to illuminate SYD. The set is a lonesome road in the middle of the desert.)*

DEADPAN CHORUS. This is Sydney Arthur. She goes by Syd.

*(***GO** *rides his bike up the road to* **SYD.***)*

DEADPAN CHORUS. Here's her only friend Go riding on his bike.
It's early evening – magic hour...

*(***GO** *stops in front of* **SYD.***)*

GO. Hey.

SYD. Hey.

GO. Got your text.

SYD. You in?

GO. I'm in. I brought provisions.

SYD. What kind of provisions?

GO. Stuff we'll need.

SYD. Like what?

GO. That's for me to know and you to find out.
Where are we going?

SYD. I was thinking here.

*(***SYD** *shows* **GO** *a flyer.)*

GO. The Manufactured Pop Star concert?

SYD. I had a dream that she knows the answer to the Meaning of Life.

DEADPAN CHORUS. This is the dream Syd had.

(**SYD** *stands facing the* **MANUFACTURED POP STAR.**)

MANUFACTURED POP STAR. Sydney A Arthur buy my new single "Meaning of Life"
It will tell you everything you need to know for only one dollar and twenty-nine cents.

SYD. You said my name.

MANUFACTURED POP STAR. Sydney A Arthur buy my new single "Meaning of Life" for only one dollar and twenty-nine cents.

SYD. This is a message.

DEADPAN CHORUS. Manufactured Pop Star disappears in a puff of smelly smoke.

GO. Her name is Manufactured Pop Star, I don't think she knows the meaning of anything.

SYD. Her name is ironic.

GO. For us. But not for her.

SYD. If you're not into it you can just go home.

GO. I'm just kidding Syd. I'm with you.

SYD. Fine. Just drive.

(**SYD** *hops onto the back of* **GO**'s *bike.*)

GO. Pedal. I'm just gonna pedal.

SYD. Fine. Whatever. Just go GO!

DEADPAN CHORUS. Cut to two and a half hours later outside the Concert.

GO. We're here.

SYD. You need to get a car.

GO. I'm working on it. I have to go park my bike. Want me to drop you off in front?

SYD. No. We have to find the backstage entrance.

GO. Do you have special tickets or something?

SYD. No I don't have tickets at all. We're gonna have to sneak in.

GO. I thought you had tickets.

SYD. I never said that.

GO. Syd, we're never gonna be able to sneak into a concert.

SYD. Not with that kind of attitude. Just follow my lead.

GO. Ok. But after I park my bike.

DEADPAN CHORUS. Three minutes and 46 seconds later. In front of Lou the Security Guard.

LOU THE SECURITY GUARD. No.

SYD. I didn't even ask anything.

LOU THE SECURITY GUARD. Yea. And the answer is no.

SYD. But –

LOU THE SECURITY GUARD. No. And if you don't walk away right now, I'm gonna have to call Security.

GO. Aren't you Security?

LOU THE SECURITY GUARD. Oh yea. Right.

SYD. You don't understand. I NEED to get inside and see Manufactured Pop Star. I had a dream about it.

LOU THE SECURITY GUARD. In that case, come on in.

SYD & GO. Seriously?

LOU THE SECURITY GUARD. Of course not! Now I'm just toying with ya.

(**ELIOT BOSSMAN** *enters.*)

ELIOT BOSSMAN. Lou stop fraternizing.

LOU THE SECURITY GUARD. Sorry Eliot. I'm disappointing you. Please don't fire me again.

ELIOT BOSSMAN. I won't. But just for that you're gonna have to work through your break.

LOU THE SECURITY GUARD. I got low blood sugar Eliot you know that.

ELIOT BOSSMAN. I don't wanna hear it. And you kids, scram. skedaddle, make like mice and -

GO. We got it the first time.

ELIOT BOSSMAN. I don't like your sass.

(**ELIOT BOSSMAN** *exits.*)

LOU THE SECURITY GUARD. If my blood sugar drops I may pass out. Last time I passed out, I woke up in Vegas married to my best friend Mary. I love Mary but I didn't wanna marry her. Now we have seven kids and a house that I've double mortgaged. I shoulda brought a snack with me tonight. Everything is starting to get fuzzy.

GO. It just so happens that I have some snacks in my bag here.

SYD. The provisions!

LOU THE SECURITY GUARD. What do you got?

GO. Not so fast. We're gonna make a trade.

DEADPAN CHORUS. This works and the two get into the concert.

Backstage at the Concert.

Syd is so close to her goal so fast.

SYD. Wow! This is so cool!

CARY THE CRAZY CREW GUY. You twos here from the union?

GO. Um, –

SYD. Yea. We're here.

CARY THE CRAZY CREW GUY. We needs you twos backstage pronto. Some kinda problem. Come ooooon.

(They start walking.)

GO. Um, we're –

SYD. Happy to help out in any way possible.

CARY THE CRAZY CREW GUY. How old are you twos, huh? You look like my sixteen year olds. I got three sixteen-year-olds – triplets. Hah! I got three sixteen-year-old girls. Ugh. Alright, justa stand here and hold onto this pipe here see? Hold on to it no matter what. alright.

(The two grab onto a pipe and hold onto it.)

GO. This is really heavy.

SYD. This is so cool.

GO. Now what?

SYD. We wait to run into Manufactured Pop Star. She tells us the meaning of life and we're home by midnight.

GO. That sounds like a very unrealistic time-table.

SYD. You're right. Maybe 12:30. I hope Jan and Martin don't notice I'm gone.

GO. I love your parents but the only thing I don't like about them is that they insist on you addressing them with their first names. It drove Max crazy.

SYD. It doesn't drive me crazy per se but it does totally annoy me. I feel like it's some weird way for them to actually avoid responsibility. If I don't call Jan Mom, she's not a Mom you know?

GO. My arms are shaking.

DEADPAN CHORUS. Speaking of Martin and Jan.

Meanwhile back at Syd's house.

(Light up on JAN and MARTIN's bedroom.)

(JAN is in bed obsessively playing some sort of competitive game on her phone. MARTIN enters.)

MARTIN. Jan.

JAN. Not now. I'm behind fifty points in one game, ahead by only ten points in another and about to beat Margery from down the street in five, four, three, two

MARTIN. Jan.

JAN. One! GOTCHA MARGERY! Try to deny that! HA!

MARTIN. Sydney isn't in her room.

JAN. Did you look downstairs? Sometimes she goes into the –

MARTIN. I looked everywhere.

JAN. Text her.

MARTIN. She's not responding.

JAN. Did we put that tracking device on her phone?

MARTIN. Good thinking.

DEADPAN CHORUS. Martin pulls his phone out of his pocket.

JAN. *(to challenger on her phone)* Ooh clever move FriedDyedFlippedtotheSide but I'm cleverer! HA! *(to*

MARTIN) What does it say?

MARTIN. Locating…locating…location unavailable.

JAN. *(stops playing)* Location unavailable?

DEADPAN CHORUS. And now a musical interlude by Manufactured Pop Star.

(Light up on **MANUFACTURED POP STAR.***)*

(Poppy synthy, dreamy sound. Autotuned.)

MANUFACTURED POP STAR. *(spoken)* Hi
This Is Manufactured Pop Star
And I Know
The Meaning Of Life

(singing)

I SEE YOU LOOKING AT ME
AND
I KNOW YOU WANNA KNOW IT
BUT IT DON'T COME FREE
YOU GOT TO
GOT TO SHOW IT
(DON'T YOU WANNA KNOW IT)

DANCE INTO THE LIGHT
I'LL SHOW YOU HOW
FREE YOURSELF GIVE ALL TO ME
RIGHT NOW

I WILL SHINE LIKE A STAR IN THE SKY
(SO BRIGHT SO BRIGHT)
I'LL SHOW YOU THE WAY
I'LL LIGHT UP YOUR DARKEST NIGHT

COME CLOSER TO ME
(OH OH OH)
DON'T BE AFRAID
IF YOU WANNA BE FREE
(OH OH OH)
YOU GOT TO BE BRAVE.

DEADPAN CHORUS. Flash forward an hour later.

Syd and Go still holding the pipe.

GO. I don't think I can hold this pipe much longer. My arms are shaking.

SYD. You should really get into better shape.

GO. I'm working on it.

SYD. Are you?

DEADPAN CHORUS. Manufactured Pop Star appears in a puff of smelly smoke

SYD. This is my moment. *(rushing to her)* Manufactured Pop Star. It's me Syd

MANUFACTURED POP STAR. I don't know you.

GO. Syd –

SYD. You came to me in a dream.

MANUFACTURED POP STAR. I love my fans.

GO. Syd I can't -

SYD. Not now GO! I don't understand your song, the Meaning of Life, like what exactly are you saying the Meaning of Life is –

MANUFACTURED POP STAR. You'll have to talk to my manager about it.

SYD. About the lyrics? It says on your website that you write all your own lyrics and –

GO. I'M LETTING GO!!! AHHHHH!!!!!!!

(**MANUFACTURED POP STAR** *starts to shake uncontrollably*)

SYD. Manufactured Pop Star are you ok?

MANUFACTURED POP STAR. *(speaking like a robot)* SYSTEM SHUT DOWN. SYSTEM OVER LOAD. BEEEEEEEP.

DEADPAN CHORUS. Manufactured Pop Star disappears in a puff of smelly smoke.
In her place stand Lou the Security Guard, Cary the Crazy Crew Guy and Eliot Bossman.

CARY THE CRAZY CREW. I told you to hold the pipe no matter what!

LOU THE SECURITY GUARD. That's how she got her steam power.

ELIOT BOSSMAN. I knew I didn't like your sass! GRAB THEM!!!!!!

(CARY and LOU rush towards SYD and GO.)

DEADPAN CHORUS. Go grabs Syd's hand and they make a run for it.

While they're running –

GO. I told you she wasn't being ironic.

SYD. I'm totally disillusioned. And disturbed. What just happened? I thought she was really speaking to me. I'm so stupid.

GO. No you're not Syd, you're the smartest person I know. I guess that's not saying much but still..

SYD. Thanks I think. I'm getting a cramp. I'm getting a cramp.

GO. We have to keep running. Just to my bike. And then we're cool.

DEADPAN CHORUS. Flash forward three minutes and forty-six seconds.

Syd is bent over in extreme pain.

GO. This is where I parked my bike. The guy said he'd watch it for me for twenty dollars.

SYD. So basically you like paid some guy to steal your bike.

GO. Yea. I did.

SYD. I guess we're walking.

DEADPAN CHORUS. Later that night on the highway.

They've been walking for some time now.

Sometimes headlights zoom by them.

Sometimes lightning is seen.

A great electrical storm is brewing.

GO. I think we took a wrong turn somewhere. None of this looks familiar.

SYD. If I got any service out here, we could see where we are.

DEADPAN CHORUS. Just then.
>   A flash of lightning.
>   Standing before them now are four strangers.

>   *(From out of nowhere,* **LOUISE, BARRY, JIMMY** *and* **MAC** *appear.)*

SYD. Whoa. Where'd you guys come from?

MAC. The desert.

BARRY. Just finished a three day vision quest.

GO. A vision quest?

BARRY. We're always trying to dig deeper into meaning.

MAC. And how it connects to nature.

LOUISE. And what is nature, you know?

GO. Right.

SYD. Yeah.

BARRY. We're storm chasers.

LOUISE. I'm Louise.

BARRY. I'm Barry.

LOUISE. That's Jimmy.

>   *(***JIMMY** *nods in their direction.)*

LOUISE. He's not a big conversationalist.

MAC. I'm Mac. I drive this crew.

SYD. I'm Syd. And this is Go. We're trying to get home before my parents figure out I'm gone. Do you think you guys could give us a lift?

MAC. Fine by me.

LOUISE. What is home, you know?

BARRY. Come on.

DEADPAN CHORUS. Twenty minutes later.
>   Inside the group's camper.
>   Full of technology.
>   Everyone is working.

GO. I'm not so sure this was the best idea Syd.

SYD. They're just taking us home – which is like maybe an hour from here and that's it. And they're cool. I like Jimmy a lot. He's like a mystery wrapped in a mystery wrapped in a mystery.

GO. He's just working that silent thing. He's not really that interesting.

SYD. Jealous much?

DEADPAN CHORUS. A doorway Syd and Go didn't see earlier opens.

Joni appears.

She's very old but very spry.

She's like a spiritual guru.

JONI. Barometer rising. Seems to be North by Northwest Mac.

MAC. Great film!

LOUISE. That's the direction of the storm Mac!

JONI. Take a strong left when you can and look up. Something big is brewing. This is our Moby Dick. My bones tell me so.

(**JONI** *exits.*)

GO. Who was that?

LOUISE. Joni.

SYD. Who's Joni?

BARRY. I ask myself that question all the time. Who is Joni? Like who is she really and why does she obsess me so?

LOUISE. She's - Just Joni. You'll see.

DEADPAN CHORUS. The radar system starts to make noises. BEEP! FLIP! WOWSA!

LOUISE. Holy MACKEREL LOOK AT THE RADAR! LOOK AT THE RADAR!

BARRY. This is the big one! This is the BIG ONE!

LOUISE. Syd, write down the numbers you see here and here – every time they change make a note. Go, do you know how to make chicken salad?

GO. Chicken salad?

LOUISE. A CHICKEN SALAD! YES A CHICKED SALAD! DID I NOT SAY CHICKEN SALAD!? Sorry, we're under a lot of pressure.

BARRY. I'll show him. Come on kid.

GO. No wait.

SYD. We need to get out of here. We're not -

LOUISE. It's dangerous out there. The storm of the millennia is forming. Safest place is in here with us.

SYD. But -

DEADPAN CHORUS. Jimmy puts his hand on Syd's shoulder.

He looks into her eyes.

She feels as if she is under some kind of jabbering spell.

SYD. *(frantically jabbering a mile a minute)* Ok. We'll stay. We're good. Hi. I'm Syd. You're Jimmy. We haven't had a chance to really talk yet. But um, anyways, so… have you ever gone skydiving? I'm dying to go. Well not really actually it terrifies me but maybe if you wanted to we could go do that together or something. What am I saying?

MAC. Hold on everyone, We're about to hit a rough -

DEADPAN CHORUS. Mac takes them off road.

It's a bumpy ride.

Everyone screams.

They fly first to the right.

Then to the left.

Then everyone does the cabbage patch.

In slow motion.

Meanwhile Jan and Martin in their car.

*(Light up on **JAN** and **MARTIN** in their car. **JAN** is feverishly playing games on her phone. **MARTIN** is driving.)*

JAN. Ooh Miss Sunnyside Up you think you're so smart but I will DOMINATE YOU, TAKE THAT!…*(nothing happens)* TAKE THAT! *(nothing happens again)* – wait

– I have no service. We just lost service. We can't lose service I was just about to –

(A great flash of lightning in the distance.)

MARTIN. Did you see that? What if Syd is out there?

(JAN starts banging the phone.)

MARTIN. *(trying to stay calm)* Jan. Please stop banging the phone.

JAN. Sometimes when I bang the phone like this, I can get service. I need to get service. I have fifteen games in rotation and I need to win all of them. I'm at the top of the food chain. I'm the queen bee, I'm –

MARTIN. YOU ARE DRIVING ME CRAZY JAN! STOP WITH THE PHONE!

Ever since – Max – you've just – all you've done is play games on your phone.

Our daughter is missing! Do you even care that Syd is missing!

JAN. Martin, of course I do.

Of course.

MARTIN. Well you haven't been showing it.

DEADPAN CHORUS. Another great flash of lightning.

Then thunder so loud it shakes the world

MARTIN. I think we should pull over until this storm passes.

DEADPAN CHORUS. The storm gets bigger.

The sound intense.

Back in the desert, the Storm Chasers and Syd and Go get ready.

(Light up on SYD, GO, MAC, LOUISE, BARRY, JIMMY and JONI.)

(SYD is holding a small video camera, GO a boom mic.)

(JIMMY holds a light. BARRY and LOUISE stand in front of the camera. JONI faces away from them all, looking up at the sky, seems like a statue. Throughout they are battling the wind – which is howling around them.)

(It should be clear that they are near the storm.)

LOUISE. Are you recording Syd?

SYD. Yea.

BARRY. Are you sure? Make sure the red button is on.

SYD. I know how to work a camera.

LOUISE. JIMMY SHINE THE LIGHT ON ME!

(**JIMMY** *does.*)

LOUISE. Are we recording?

SYD. YES!

LOUISE. Alright then someone count me in.

BARRY. I can't. I'm on camera.

GO. Three. Two. One. Action.

LOUISE. HELLO FELLOW STORM CHASERS EVERYWHERE
I'M LOUISE BRACKENBURGER and –

BARRY. I'M BARRY MARGOLOPEZMATA.

LOUISE. WE ARE DEEP IN THE DESERT WHERE -

(**GO**'s *Boom Mic hits* **LOUISE** *in the head.*)

(She falls to the ground.)

LOUISE. Oh my stars!

GO. I'm so sorry. I was holding it like you said and then it just – slipped.

BARRY. You have to be more focused! Both of you! This is no joking matter. This is our life's work.

SYD. *(cracking under the pressure)* We didn't ask to be out here! We didn't ask for any of this!

LOUISE. Yes you did. You asked for a ride!

MAC. This is part of the RIDE!
YEEEEEEEEEEEEHAWWWWWWWWWWW!!!!!!
MOTHER NATURE!!!!!!!!!!!!!!!!!

DEADPAN CHORUS. Lightning.
More lightning.
Even more Lightning.

JONI. *(with her back turned)* She's started.

GO. This is so rad.

SYD. I don't feel very safe out here.

(**JIMMY** *puts his hand on* **SYD***'s shoulder.*)

(mile a minute) I feel safe now. Do you come out here often? This is my first time. I mean I've been out in the desert but never in the midst of an electrical storm and – oh my goodness you smell like fresh buns right out of the oven! This gushing is so not like me. I'm not like this at all.

LOUISE. Are you filming this Syd?

DEADPAN CHORUS. Syd remembers that she's supposed to be filming.

SYD. Oh yea.

DEADPAN CHORUS. She realizes she has no idea where the camera is.

SYD. Huh.

DEADPAN CHORUS. She starts to look for the camera.

Joni falls into some kind of trance-like state.

Syd is transfixed.

(A huge reverberating drum beat sounds.)

(Then music.)

JONI.
OH SKY
OH HEAVEN
OH MOON
OH LIGHT
OH POWER

OH ME
OH MY
OH WE
OH WHY
OH FREE

(beckoning the others to get closer to her, forming a circle of power, hands lifted high to the heavens)

COME CLOSER TO ME
DON'T BE AFRAID
IF YOU WANT TO BE FREE
YOU GOT TO BE BRAVE

(Another huge beat. Then the electrical storm starts.)

(During it JAN and MARTIN get out of their car and watch it.)

(After it's over...)

JAN. Martin, I think we should go see what's out there.

(When the storm is done, JONI turns around and sits with her back to everyone. MAC, BARRY, JIMMY and GO start putting equipment away.)

MAC. You were good out there kid.

BARRY. Real good. Never saw someone take to it as fast as you did.

GO. I've never felt more alive.

MAC. Looks like you've been bit.

GO. Bit?

BARRY. He just means – You're gonna be chasing that feeling the rest of your life now.

MAC. You should chase with us Go..

BARRY. Become part of the crew.

We got room.

(GO looks at MAC, BARRY and JIMMY.)

MAC. Let's eat some chicken salad.

(He hands each a container and a fork.)

(They start to eat.)

MAC. Mighty fine chicken salad.

BARRY. Mighty fine.

DEADPAN CHORUS. Go is surprised to find himself glowing with happiness.

Syd on the other hand...

(*Light up on* **SYD** *and* **LOUISE**, *who's holding a chicken salad sandwich.*)

LOUISE. Tell me you got all of that on video Syd.

SYD. Um, well, I think I did but at some point I don't know if –

LOUISE. Give me the camera.

SYD. Yea, ok. Well, that's what I was trying to say. I was looking for it but it's nowhere. It's like vanished.

LOUISE. You're gonna have to tell Joni. I'm not telling her that.

SYD. Ok.

LOUISE. Now.

SYD. Ok.

LOUISE. And give her this chicken salad sandwich.

(**SYD** *gets up.*)

DEADPAN CHORUS. Syd stands for some time behind Joni.
Thinking Joni knows she's there.
Finally.

(**SYD** *stands behind* **JONI**.)

SYD. Um Joni?

JONI. …

SYD. I brought you this chicken salad sandwich.

(**SYD** *slides it in front of* **JONI** *who starts eating it like an animal.*)

SYD. I'm Syd. We never – officially – um, so I was supposed to video your – um, what just happened and the camera it like – um, I lost the camera and –

JONI. …

SYD. So I just wanted to tell you that. Well I didn't really want to tell you that but Louise made me. Louise acts like she's cool but she's kind of abrasive actually. I also just wanted to let you know that what happened tonight was totally amazing. I mean, I don't even really understand what happened but it made me feel so much and I think it changed me – like now I think more things than I thought are possible, I don't know if that makes sense but anyways, thanks.

(Beat.)

JONI. ...you're still standing there.

SYD. Right. I know. Um, I just wanted to make sure that in the morning you guys could like drop us off back out our houses.

JONI. I had a house once. It had four walls. And a ceiling. But it never kept me warm.

SYD. Oh right well I mean I don't really understand like – I'm not like, so..

JONI. Stop jammering. And speak direct.

SYD. I had a dream. But the dream wasn't real. And now I don't know what I'm supposed to do.

JONI. About what?

SYD. About anything.

JONI. Then don't do anything.

SYD. You mean like just like –

JONI. Stop. And listen. And breathe. Everyone always forgets about breathing. Everyone always forgets about listening.

DEADPAN CHORUS. Syd rolls her eyes.

She thinks Joni is a cheeseball.

She hates when people say things like that.

JONI. You are afraid of your silence.

DEADPAN CHORUS. This makes Syd mad.

She makes a decision.

Back to Jan and Martin, in the desert.

Closer to Syd than they realize, looking for the light.

MARTIN. I'm certain it was this way. But everything is starting to look the same.

JAN. Martin I'm worried that I'm about to lose myself. We can't lose another child.

(JAN*'s breath seems to be getting erratic.*)

MARTIN. *(trying to calm her down)* Remember when we used to take yoga together?

JAN. I remember.

MARTIN. That was fun. All four of us in yoga class.

JAN. Uh uh.

MARTIN. How'd those classes always start?

JAN. *(hard time talking, out of breath at first)* We'd *(gasp)* have *(gasp)* to *(gasp)* get *(gasp)* mats.

MARTIN. Yea but fast forward to when class started and Patrizia would start talking. What'd she say?

(**PATRIZIA**, *a tough but loving yoga teacher from Italy appears.*)

(*As she instructs,* **SYD**, **MARTIN** *and* **SYD***'s brother* **MAX** *appear and sit down for class.* **SYD** *and* **MAX** *make faces at each other throughout.*)

(*We've gone back in time.*)

JAN.	PATRIZIA.
Close *(gasp)* Your *(gasp)*	CLOSE YOUR EYES.

PATRIZIA. And now. Get comfortable. And breathe.
Breathing is where you all screw it up.
Everyone wants to show me you're breathing.
No.
I know you breathe.
You are alive.
You are here.
You paid for my class.
If you haven't paid for my class, get out!
Now I'll be quiet.

(*For a brief moment all is calm.*)

(**MAX** *farts.* **SYD** *and* **MARTIN** *start to giggle.*)

JAN. It's not funny.
We're supposed to be meditating.

MAX. Meditating makes me gassy.

SYD. I have to stop. The smell. I can't.

MARTIN. I'm with Syd.

MAX. You guys love my aroma.

JAN. Ok. It's enough. All three of you. We are going to – oh wow Max that smell. Nope. Can't handle this.
Let's go eat.

SYD & MAX. Can we invite Go?

DEADPAN CHORUS. At a TGI Fridays.
The family with Go.

MAX. Jan you have to come see me and Go in the Talent Show this year.

SYD. You guys are really doing it?

MAX & GO. Uh huh.

JAN. Doing what?

MAX & GO. Funky Cold Medina.

MARTIN. The Tone Loc masterpiece? I love that song. "Hi my name is Tina"...

SYD. Martin, you are so embarrassing.

MARTIN. That's part of my job as your parent.

(JAN *has started to cry.*)

SYD.	**MARTIN.**
Why are you crying?	Everything alright?

JAN. I'm just so happy that we're all together right now. You too Go. You know you're part of our family too.

GO. Thanks Jan.

JAN. I'm just so happy.

DEADPAN CHORUS. Back to the present.
Syd and Go find each other.

SYD & GO. I've been looking for you. I need to talk. You go first. You go.

SYD.	**GO.**
We have to leave here.	The guys asked me to stay and I'm gonna.

SYD. Wait. What?

GO. I want to stay Syd. I've been kind of lost since school ended and…since Max and this is the first time I'm feeling – good, you know?

SYD. But I need you Go.

GO. You don't need me. I just remind you of Max.

SYD. You were his best friend.

GO. You were his sister.

(Beat.)

DEADPAN CHORUS. The two miss Max so much it practically drips off them like sweat.

SYD. I was sitting with him having breakfast. He farted. We laughed. Then this strange look came over his face. He said –

(MAX appears.)

MAX. Oh. Wow. Syd, I –

(MAX disappears.)

SYD. And then he – and ever since then I don't know what anything means anymore.

DEADPAN CHORUS. Syd turns away from Go

She turns towards the darkness.

Before she's gotten too far, Jimmy catches up to her.

SYD. Oh.

Hey.

(JIMMY takes his coat off and hands it to SYD.)

JIMMY. Keep warm.

(JIMMY kisses her on the cheek, then disappears into the darkness.)

DEADPAN CHORUS. That was Syd's first real kiss.

Even if it was only on the cheek.

Soon after Syd, tired, sits down on the sand and closes her eyes.

Here are the thoughts in her head.

SYD. I wish you were here Max.

I wish you would speak to me.

I wish you would tell me it's ok

I wish you were here.

I wish you were here.

I wish you were here.

DEADPAN CHORUS. But Max can't speak to her now.

He can't show up.

Syd acknowledges this silence.

She begins to cry.

(JAN *and* MARTIN *appear in front of* SYD.)

JAN & MARTIN. Syd?

SYD. How did you –

JAN. It's really you! You're ok. You're ok.

SYD. I'm ok.

MARTIN. What happened?

SYD. Can we talk about it later?

JAN. Of course. Of course.

DEADPAN CHORUS. Go can't sleep that night.

He doesn't even try.

He looks up at the stars.

(Somehow the sky should illuminate stars. Wide open sky.)

(GO *lies in the desert, looking up.*)

DEADPAN CHORUS. He sees a new life ahead of him.

GO. Anything in the world is possible.

Anything at all.

DEADPAN CHORUS. Back on the road.

Martin drives.

Jan looks out the window.

Syd sits in the back.

Jan turns around and looks at her daughter.

JAN. Where'd you get that jacket?

SYD. This guy. I don't know. He's cool.

JAN. It's cute.

MARTIN. We were so worried about you last night. When that electrical storm started…

SYD. I was really close to it. But I was safe.

(Silence. They're just driving for a moment.)

JAN. *(looking out the window)* I grew up near the ocean and I lived through a terrible hurricane. Everything in my neighborhood was destroyed. I'd walk the streets I grew up on and get lost because all the landmarks were leveled. All the trees down. Except for this one tall thin tree. A tree I hadn't really noticed before. It stood. It survived. And I remember wondering – was it supposed to survive or was it completely random?

SYD. What'd you decide?

JAN. I didn't.

(Beat.)

MARTIN. I'm hungry. Who's hungry?

DEADPAN CHORUS. The three drive off into the sunrise
Towards a diner they favor
Near where they live.
The End.

(End of play.)

Why Aren't You Dead Already

Halley Feiffer

WHY AREN'T YOU DEAD ALREADY was first presented by Keen Company (Jonathan Silverstein, Artistic Director; Mark Armstrong, Director of New Work) and Samuel French, Inc. as part of the 2014 Keen Teens Festival of New Work. The performance was directed by Liz Carlson, with sets by Colin McGurk costumes by Ricola Wille, lights by Jeffrey Toombs, and original music and sound design by M. Florian Staab. The Production Stage Manager was Ryan Parow. The cast was as follows:

MARSHALL	Christian Benenati
THERESA	Daniella Campos
MIMI	Kimberly McBride
GARRET	Marcus Edward
PETER	Ralphie Irizzary
ANNA	Erin Leong
AUGUST	Michael Alexander Lopez
MALLORY	Zoe Marcel
CHRIS	Devante Rowe
LIZ	Shanique Williams

CHARACTERS

ANNA – 15. Mousy, cute, quiet.

CHRIS – 16. Jocky, handsome, loud.

MALLORY – 16. Pretty, perky, mean.

TERESA – 15. What Mallory is.

LIZ – Anna's mother. 40. Beautiful, delicate, terrified.

PETER – Anna's father. 40. Handsome, stoic, terrified.

MARSHALL – 16. Pimply, pugnacious, cruel.

GARRETT – 15. What Marshall is.

MIMI – Mallory's mother. 40. Beautiful, fierce, terrified.

AUGUST – Marshall's father. 40. What Mimi is.

SETTING

A suburban American town.

TIME

Today.

PRODUCTION NOTES

Design elements should be minimal – only the necessary elements need be present (e.g. 2 table, some chairs, a sandwich, etc).

The scenes between Anna and Chris in the cafeteria can have a warm, romantic tone in their design elements – think the soda fountain scene in *Our Town*.

The interrogation scenes, in contrast, can have a cold, scary, sinister tone – think *Law & Order: Special Victims Unit*.

ACKNOWLEDGMENTS

Thank you to Keen Company, for commissioning this play.

SCENE 1.

*(**ANNA** and **CHRIS** sit in their high school's cafeteria, at adjacent tables.)*

(They are alone.)

*(**CHRIS** wears a lacrosse jersey and sweatpants. He eats a salami sandwich and has a half-drunk bottle of Diet Pepsi on the table in front of him. There is a lacrosse stick propped up against the table, next to him. He sits with his legs spread open and munches, enthusiastically.)*

*(**ANNA** wears a wool dress and thick tights. She reads a book, and has a Ziploc bag of mini carrot sticks in front of her on the table. She sits hunched over, as if she is trying to take up the least amount of space possible, and very slowly places one carrot stick at a time into her mouth as she pores over her book.)*

*(**CHRIS** watches **ANNA** for a moment.)*

(She does not notice.)

(He takes a big gulp of Diet Coke, still watching her.)

(He burps.)

(She does not notice.)

(He watches her.)

(A beat. Then –)

CHRIS. What do you play?

*(**ANNA** looks up at **CHRIS**.)*

(A beat. Then –)

(She looks back down at her book.)

CHRIS. WHAT DO YOU PLAY?

> (**CHRIS** *takes a big bite of his sandwich.*)

ANNA. *(looks up at Chris again)* What? Oh! You're –

> *(looks around)*

– you're...talking to...

> *(looks around; breathlessly)*

...me...?

> (**CHRIS** *laughs, his mouth full of food.*)

CHRIS. Do you see anyone else here?

> (**ANNA** *smiles, nervously.*)

ANNA. *(softly)* No-o....
CHRIS. *(chewing)* So what do you play???
ANNA. Oh. I...don't...
CHRIS. What?
ANNA. I...don't...understand...?

> *(beat)*

The question.

> (**CHRIS** *laughs. Indicates his lacrosse stick.*)

CHRIS. Sports? What *sport* do you –
ANNA. Oh!

> *(laughs)*

Oh. I don't.

> *(Beat.)*

CHRIS. Whaddayou mean?
ANNA. I don't...

> *(beat)*

...play...?

> *(Beat.)*

CHRIS. *(incredulous)* Anything???

ANNA. *(nods, matter-of-factly)* Anything.

*(Beat. **CHRIS** looks at her like she is an alien.)*

CHRIS. Sooo...what do you *do*??

(She laughs.)

ANNA. I...

(indicates her book)

...read...? And I...write...?

(Beat.)

CHRIS. That's it?

(A beat. She thinks.)

ANNA. I guess.

(A beat. He thinks. Takes another bite of his sandwich. Chews. Thinks.)

CHRIS. So your parents don't *make* you? Play a sport???

ANNA. *(shrugs)* Not...really....

*(**CHRIS** takes off his lacrosse jersey, revealing a tight-fitting Hanes tee-shirt.)*

*(**ANNA** looks for a second, then looks down at her book.)*

CHRIS. *(shakes his head)* Man. My dad would fucking kill me.

ANNA. *(looks down at her book)* I don't think my dad would notice, either way.

CHRIS. *(chews)* You're lucky, man.

(A beat. She smiles, sheepishly.)

ANNA. *(lifting her eyes toward him)* You don't...like...? Playing...sports...???

(A beat. He thinks.)

CHRIS. Idunno. I never really thought about it.

ANNA. *(laughs)* That's funny.

CHRIS. Why?

ANNA. *(with a sort of breathless laugh)* 'Cause you play...so many...!

CHRIS. *(putting his sandwich down)* How do you know?!

(**ANNA**'s *face turns red. She looks down at her book.*)

ANNA. *(softly)* I don't know.

CHRIS. *(teasing)* Are you *stalking* me?!

ANNA. *(face turning even redder)* No-o-o...!

CHRIS. *(laughing)* Relax! I'm just teasing.

(She looks up, sheepishly.)

ANNA. Oh-h-h....

(He looks at her. Smiles.)

(She looks at him. Smiles a little, too.)

(A beat. Then –)

CHRIS. *(biting into his sandwich)* I know everyone knows everything about me.

ANNA. *(unsure of what to say)* You – you d-do...?

CHRIS. Hells yeah!

(takes a big bite out of his sandwich)

I'm the tenth grade class president! Everyone knows my business.

(chews, contentedly)

I don't mind.

(chews, musingly)

I like it, kinda.

(A beat. He chews. **ANNA** *looks down at her book. Then, she closes it. Looks up at him.)*

ANNA. I can't imagine it.

CHRIS. *(mouth full of food)* What.

ANNA. Everyone...knowing...all your business. All the time.

CHRIS. Yeah, no one knows anything about you!

ANNA. *(looking down at her book)* Ohhh....

CHRIS. You're like a ninja!

ANNA. *(face growing red)* ...I don't...kn-kno-o-ow....

CHRIS. You're like an invisible little ninja...!

ANNA. *(almost inaudible)* ...oh-k-ka-ay....

CHRIS. *(laughing; oblivious)* You're like an invisible little quiet little nothing little NINJA!

(He laughs, mouth full of food.)

(ANNA starts to cry.)

(He notices.)

CHRIS. Oh – oh no!

(She cries.)

What's wrong?!

(She cries.)

ANNA. *(wiping her nose)* I – I'm s-sorry, I –

CHRIS. *I'm* sorry. I made you cry! Oh my god....

ANNA. *(wiping her eyes)* No, n-no-o, it's –

CHRIS. I've never made a girl *cry* before....

ANNA. It's not you, it's –

CHRIS. *(very alarmed)* What's *wrong?!*

ANNA. I –

(beat; she cries)

– sometimes, I – I just...can't...

(beat)

...Someone...*says*...something – something totally innocuous, something that doesn't even *mean anything*, and it just – it makes me...*feel* something – I suddenly... feel...very...*alone*...and – and...*different*...from everyone else.... And I just...start...*crying*...and I just can't....

(She cries.)

...I can't...*stop*...!

(A beat. He nods compassionately.)

CHRIS. I know what you mean.

ANNA. *(wiping her nose)* No you don't.

CHRIS. Okay, I don't, really. But... I *want* to....

   (A beat.)

   (Then –)

CHRIS. Here.

   (He hands ANNA his lacrosse jersey.)

   (She looks up. Looks at the jersey.)

   (A beat. Then –)

ANNA. What is this?

CHRIS. My lacrosse jersey.

   (beat; as if it's totally obvious)

To wipe your nose.

ANNA. Oh.

   (A beat.)

   (They both look at the lacrosse jersey. Then –)

   *(**ANNA** starts to laugh.)*

ANNA. *(laughing, through tears)*

I don't want to wipe my nose with that...!

   (Chis looks at the lacrosse jersey.)

   (A beat. Then –)

   (He starts to laugh, too.)

CHRIS. *(laughing)* Oh yeah!

ANNA. *(laughing)* That's – gross...!

CHRIS. *(laughing)* Yeah, it totally is!

ANNA. *(laughing, sort of breathlessly)* Why would you hand me that...? To wipe my nose...with...?!!

CHRIS. *(cracking up)* I don't know!!!

   (They laugh and laugh and laugh.)

   (They calm down. Stop laughing. Look at each other. They smile.)

(A beat. Then –)

CHRIS. I'm Chris.

ANNA. I know.

CHRIS. You are...?

ANNA. Oh! Anna. I'm Anna.

CHRIS. *(smiles)* It's nice to meet you, Anna.

ANNA. *(smiles)* It's nice to meet you, Chris.

(They smile at each other.)

(A beat. Then –)

CHRIS. *(indicating the jersey)* Now, wipe your nose with this jersey or I'll hit you with my lacrosse stick.

(She laughs.)

CHRIS. *(playfully)* I'm serious! Why are you laughing?! I'll pick up my lacrosse stick and I'll smack you over the head!!!

(She laughs.)

CHRIS. *(laughing)* I'm serious! You wanna watch me?!?

(He picks up the lacrosse stick and pretends to hit her with it.)

(She laughs and laughs and laughs.)

(So does he.)

CHRIS. *(mock-hitting **ANNA** on one side of her body with the lacrosse stick)* Take *that!* And *that!!* And *that!!!*

(She laughs and laughs and laughs.)

(So does he.)

CHRIS. *(mock-hitting her on the other side of her body)*

Now the *other* side! *Boom! BOOM!! BOOM!!!*

(She laughs and laughs and laughs as he mock-hits her. So does he.)

(Then –)

(She grabs the lacrosse stick.)

(He holds on to the other end of the stick. Stops mock-hitting her.)

(They both just hold on to the stick.)

(She looks him dead in the eyes.)

(He looks her dead in the eyes, back.)

(They look at each other.)

(A beat.)

(A beat.)

(The electricity between them is palpable, penetrative – almost painful.)

(A beat.)

(Then –)

(Blackout.)

SCENE 2.

(MALLORY and TERESA sit facing the audience. A bright light shines on their faces.)

(MALLORY wears a tight-fitting velour track suit. TERESA wears the same.)

(MALLORY chews gum. TERESA twirls her hair.)

MALLORY. Yeah it doesn't really make any sense –

TERESA. Yeah like it doesn't really make any *sense* –

MALLORY. Like we would never try to like *hurt* anyone –

TERESA. Oh yeah like we would never, totally *never* –

MALLORY. Like we just wanna have *fun* –

TERESA. Yeah like we just totally just wanna have *fun* –

MALLORY. Like we just wanna fuck around –

TERESA. Yeah like fucking around is just our *thing* –

MALLORY. *(snapping her gum)* Wait can you say "fuck" in here???

TERESA. *(stopping twirling her hair)* Wait like yeah can you???

(They listen.)

(A beat. Then –)

MALLORY. 'K cool.

TERESA. 'K yeah like cool then thanks.

MALLORY. But like yeah like I don't really understand like what the big *deal* is –

TERESA. Yeah like me *neither* –

MALLORY. Like if someone is depressed then like I'm *sorry* –

TERESA. Yeah like totally yeah me *too* –

MALLORY. But like I'm not responsible for the *decisions* they make –

TERESA. Oh no yeah totally yeah me *neither* –

MALLORY. Like if you wanna hate your life then like be my *guest* –

TERESA. Yeah like totally be mine *too* –

MALLORY. Like if you wanna be a slut and a whore then like who am I to *stop* you???

TERESA. Right like totally me too *also* –

MALLORY. I mean I know that sounds *harsh*, but like –

TERESA. *Yeah* but like –

MALLORY. Like if you wanna write a fucking note to your like *parents* and like that's *it* 'cause like you have no *friends* or whatever and like climb up to the top of the fucking *water tower* and then like *jump off* and <u>*die*</u> –

TERESA. Yeah.

MALLORY. – *at <u>fifteen</u>* –

TERESA. Yeah.

MALLORY. – then like – *go* for it, you know??? Like who am I to *say* –

TERESA. Yeah *totally* –

MALLORY. *(sharply turning to Teresa)* I'm <u>TALKING, TERESA</u>.

(A beat.)

*(**TERESA**'s face flushes.)*

(She looks down at her hands.)

TERESA. *(softly)* Sorry, Mallory.

MALLORY. *(snapping her gum with irritation)* Ugh what was I saying???

(She listens.)

(A beat.)

MALLORY. Yeah like that was pretty much it.

(beat)

Like, I'm sorry she *died*. Of *course* I am.

(beat)

I'm not a *monster*.

(beat)

But like... I don't understand what *we* have to do with it.

(A beat.)

TERESA. *(head down; softly)* Yeah like totally yeah me neither.

(They listen. **MALLORY** *chews gum.)*

*(***TERESA*** twirls her hair.)*

(A beat. Then –)

MALLORY.	**TERESA.**
Can we go now???	Can we go now???

(Blackout.)

SCENE 3.

(LIZ and PETER sit facing the audience. A bright light shines on their faces.)

(LIZ has dark circles under her eyes. She pulls anxiously at her hair as she speaks.)

(PETER wears a suit. He sits very still and speaks very slowly, softly and deliberately.)

LIZ. *(pulling at her hair)* I don't understand why we have to do this to*gether*....

PETER. *(gently)* Don't question them, Liz.

LIZ. *(shrilly)* Don't tell me what to *do*, Peter! You're not my *husband!* Anymore.

(PETER sighs.)

LIZ. *(pulling at her hair)* Why are you – *sighing?!* Like that?!?

PETER. *(in a measured tone)* Liz.

LIZ. *(hysterical)* Why are you – saying my...*name?!* Like that?!?

(LIZ starts to cry.)

(PETER sighs.)

(LIZ pulls at her hair, hysterically, as she sobs.)

(PETER runs his fingers through his hair. He sighs.)

(A beat. Then –)

PETER. *(to the unseen interrogator; gently)* I think we might... need a break.

LIZ. *(sobbing into her hands)* I don't need *anything*...!

(sobbing)

I just need...

(sobs)

...my *daughter*...!

(cries)

...back...!

(She sobs.)

*(****PETER*** *mops his brow.)*

(A beat. Then –)

*(****LIZ*** *wipes her eyes, lifts her head from her hands, and sits up. She looks out at the audience, her face swollen and red.)*

LIZ. *(wiping her nose; softly)* I'm ready.

PETER. Great.

LIZ. *(whipping around on Peter)* What?! Why are you saying *"great"* like that?!? I don't need you to *approve <u>everything I do</u>!!!*

(A beat. **PETER** *mops his brow.)*

PETER. *(measured)* Liz...

(Suddenly, **LIZ** *hurls herself onto* **PETER**. *Throws her arms around him. Sobs, onto his shoulder.)*

*(****PETER*** *watches, uncomfortably.)*

(A beat. Then –)

(He puts his arm around her, tentatively. He holds her, awkwardly. He lets her sob into him.)

LIZ. *(sobbing)* She's – *gone*, Peter...!

PETER. *(gently)* I know.

LIZ. She's never coming *back*...!

PETER. *(softly)* I know, Lizzie. I know.

LIZ. And we're – still here...!

(sobs)

And she's just – *gone...!*

PETER. *(rubbing Liz's arm)* I know. I know.

*(****LIZ*** *cries. She cries.* **PETER** *holds her.)*

LIZ. *(to the unseen interrogator)* Do you know what it said? The text?? That made her do it???

(beat; cries)

LIZ. *(cont.)* It said: *"Why aren't you dead already?"*

Did you know that's what it said???

(beat; almost to herself)

"Why aren't you dead already?"....

(beat; looks up)

They'd been saying it to her...for weeks. Texting. Facebooking. Snapchatting. All that shit. All these kids. These kids, who are...so...*sick.*

(She shakes her head. Cries.)

(A beat. Then –)

PETER. Who...*says*...such a thing? To another...*person?*

(beat; shakes his head)

Who...*writes*...such a thing? And then – hits *"Send"?*

(beat; he thinks)

Wouldn't you hit *"Delete"*...?

(A beat. She shakes her head.)

(LIZ *looks at him, with something like love.)*

(They both cry.)

PETER. *(shaking his head; softly)* I could see myself writing something...like that.... When I was a kid, I guess. When I was a stupid, little...arrogant, little...fucking *brat,* and I...

(He trails off. He thinks. He shakes his head.)

PETER. But then – wouldn't I...just hit *"Delete"???*

(shakes his head)

I wouldn't hit *"Send"....*

(shakes his head)

How could you hit *"Send"*...???

(shakes his head)

Just hit *"Delete"*...!

(shakes his head; cries)

Delete...!

PETER.	**LIZ.**
Delete.	Delete.

(He stops shaking his head. He stares at the air in front of him.)

(His eyes become dead.)

(LIZ looks at PETER.)

(A beat. Then –)

(She takes his hand.)

(He looks at her with something like love.)

(A beat. Then –)

(Blackout.)

SCENE 4.

(**ANNA** *and* **CHRIS** *hang out in* **CHRIS**' *bedroom.*)

(**ANNA** *wears a long-sleeved shirt underneath a wool jumper.* **CHRIS** *wears his lacrosse jersey.*)

(*They are in the middle of a playful fooling-around session.*)

CHRIS. (*trying to kiss Anna*) ...why won't you let me...?!

ANNA. (*not letting him kiss her; laughing*) Because you smell like bacon...!

CHRIS. (*trying to kiss her again; laughing*) No I don't...!

ANNA. (*not letting him kiss her; laughing*) You just ate that bacon and egg sandwich...!

CHRIS. (*trying to kiss her; laughing*) So...?!

ANNA. (*not letting him kiss her; laughing*) So...?!? I'm a *vegetarian*...!

CHRIS. (*trying to kiss her; laughing*) But you *love* me...!

ANNA. (*not letting him kiss her; laughing*) But I don't love bacon and *eggs*...!

CHRIS. (*trying to kiss her; laughing*) *Everyone* loves bacon and eggs!!!

ANNA. (*laughing*) Well... I *don't*...!

CHRIS. (*laughing*) Why?!

ANNA. Because I'm...

(*beat; she stops laughing*)

...different.

(*She pulls away from him.*)

(*He keeps laughing. Then –*)

(*He notices she is not.*)

CHRIS. Hey. *Hey.*

ANNA. (*looking away from him; softly*) What.

CHRIS. What's wrong?

ANNA. *(softly)* I don't know.

CHRIS. *(very, very gently)* Tell me, babe.

ANNA. No-o....

CHRIS. *(sweetly; playfully) Tell* me, babe...!

(He tickles her.)

ANNA. *(smiling)* No-o-o...!

He tickles her harder. She laughs.

CHRIS. *(laughing; tickling) Tell me, babe!!!*

(CHRIS moves his hand to ANNA's arm – she violently pulls it away.)

ANNA. Chris!

(Beat. She looks away from him.)

(Holds her arm.)

CHRIS. Anna....

(beat)

Show me.

(A beat. Then –)

(ANNA reluctantly holds out her arm.)

(CHRIS very gently pulls her sleeve up...revealing a bandage on her wrist.)

CHRIS. Anna...why...?

ANNA. *(softly)* I don't know.

CHRIS. Again...???

ANNA. I can't...*talk* about it...! Chris.

CHRIS. Please, baby. *Tell* me.

ANNA. *(shaking her head)* You can't under*stand* it, Chris....

CHRIS. Why *not*...?

ANNA. 'Cause – you're *popular*. You have *everything*. Everyone *knows* you. Everyone's *nice* to you.

CHRIS. Ohhh....

ANNA. I'm – *nothing*.

(beat)

ANNA. *(cont.)* I'm nothing.

CHRIS. *(reaching for her again)* That's not *true*, baby....

ANNA. Don't touch me.

CHRIS. I'm sorry.

(They sit in silence, not looking at each other.)

(A beat. Then –)

ANNA. I know I'm not *nothing*.

CHRIS. Okay....

ANNA. But people treat me like I'm nothing.

CHRIS. Anna....

ANNA. They say horrible things to me.

(Beat.)

And it makes me want to die.

CHRIS. But why can't you just tell them to fuck off?

ANNA. Because – I *can't*, Chris...! I'm not like you. I can't.

CHRIS. Well then I'll tell them *for* you!

ANNA. *(becoming hysterical)* That'll just make it *worse!*

CHRIS. But you can't keep – just...*doing*...this...!

(She hangs her head.)

ANNA. I know.

CHRIS. So – we have to...*do*...something...!

ANNA. I think...we just...wait.

CHRIS. Wait?

ANNA. Wait. 'Til...high school is over. 'Til we're free.

CHRIS. But –

ANNA. But what?

CHRIS. But what do we do in the meantime?

*(**ANNA** thinks.)*

(A beat. Then –)

ANNA. *(with a small smile)* Kiss.

*(**CHRIS** looks at **ANNA**. He smiles a sad smile.)*

(A beat. Then –)

(He leans in to kiss her.)

(Before he can –)

(Blackout.)

SCENE 5.

(MARSHALL and GARRETT sit facing the audience. A bright light shines on their faces.)

(MARSHALL wears an oversized hoodie and an oversized baseball cap.)

(GARRETT wears the same.)

(MARSHALL zips his hoodie up and down. GARRETT fidgets with his baseball cap.)

MARSHALL. It was a *joke*, man.

GARRETT. Yeah, it was a *joke*.

MARSHALL. Everyone takes their shit so *seriously*, man..

GARRETT. Yeah, it's like, you never heard of a *joke*??

MARSHALL. People take them*selves* so seriously....

GARRETT. Yeah, it's like, lighten *up*, you know???

MARSHALL. People don't know how to have *fun*.

GARRETT. Yeah, it's like, where the *party* at, right?!?

MARSHALL. People forget what the *point* is, man.

GARRETT. Yeah, people forget why we're *here*.

MARSHALL. They forget we're here to have *fun*, man.

GARRETT. Yeah, we're on this planet to live and have *fun!*

MARSHALL. So if I send you a text that's just for *fun*, man, like –

GARRETT. Have *fun* with it!

MARSHALL. Right! Have *fun* with it. Right. Am I right?

GARRETT. You're right! Man, you're *right*.

MARSHALL. I'm right. I'm *right*. And like, if she didn't wanna have fun –

GARRETT. Right, then like –

MARSHALL. – then like she shouldn't have been going around sucking all those *dicks*, am I right?

GARRETT. You're right, man! You're –

(The unseen interrogator says something. They listen.)

(A beat. Then –)

MARSHALL.   **GARRETT.**
  Whose dicks?   *Whose* dicks?

(Beat.)

GARRETT. Well, Chris.

MARSHALL. Yeah.

GARRETT. And like...

(A beat. They think.)

MARSHALL. I guess that's...it.

GARRETT. Yeah, I guess just Chris.

MARSHALL. But like – that's a big *deal.*

GARRETT. Yeah, like, that's *Chris.*

MARSHALL. 'Cause like, man, dating Chris? Is like –

GARRETT. Oh yeah, it's like –

MARSHALL. It's like the holy *grail,* man!

GARRETT. Yeah, like uncharted *territory,* man.

MARSHALL. Yeah, like Chris is un*touchable,* man.

GARRETT. Yeah. Like...yeah.

MARSHALL. Like that playa don't date *anyone,* you know what I'm sayin'?

GARRETT. Nah, man, like <u>no one.</u>

MARSHALL. Like, he'll fuck *around,* don't get me wrong.

GARRETT. Yeah, like fucking around is just his *thing.*

MARSHALL. But like, with some *slut,* or something. Like Mallory....

GARRETT. Right, like Mallory, or *Teresa*...

MARSHALL. Right, like *Teresa,* but like, he'll never –

GARRETT. – no, never –

MARSHALL. Like he'll never...like...*date* a girl. Like, seriously.

(beat; thinks)

Like...ever.

GARRETT. No, like...*never.*

MARSHALL. That's why –

GARRETT. – yeah, like –

MARSHALL. – that's why it was so *crazy*, like...when he chose – *her*....

  (beat)

  You know???

GARRETT. Yeah, 'cause like –

MARSHALL. 'Cause it was like...

  (Beat.)

  (Beat.)

  (Beat.)

MARSHALL.	**GARRETT.**
Why???	*Why???*

  (They laugh.)

MARSHALL. Like, she's *nobody*...you know??

GARRETT. Yeah, and like –

MARSHALL. And like, a *loser*, you know???

GARRETT. Yeah, and like –

MARSHALL. And like, she doesn't even play any sports. Like, she doesn't even do really *anything*. Except, like, sit in the cafe*teria*.

  And like...*read*. And like...

GARRETT. Eat carrots.

MARSHALL. Right, eat *carrots*.

  (beat)

  And that's it.

GARRETT. Yeah that's *it*.

MARSHALL. And like, no one even knows who she *is*, and like –

GARRETT. – and like –

MARSHALL. – and like she's not even *hot*. Like, *at all*.

GARRETT. Yeah, like not *at all!*

MARSHALL. And like... I heard she was a *virgin*. Before –
GARRETT. Yeah me too I heard that *too*.
MARSHALL. So that means, like –
GARRETT. – yeah, like –
MARSHALL. Like, she wasn't even that *good*.
GARRETT. Right.
MARSHALL. Like, she had no *moves*.
GARRETT. *(laughing)* Yeah, no *moves!*
MARSHALL. Like, she probably just...*laid*...there.
GARRETT. Right. Just like –

(He does an imitation of a girl just laying there.)

(They laugh.)

MARSHALL. So like, I don't get it. Chris cashed in his chips for a girl who wasn't even that hot and who didn't even know how to fuck, even.
GARRETT. Word, yo.

(They laugh.)

(A beat. Then –)

MARSHALL. But I guess if you took all her clothes off, like I guess she'd have a nice *body* probably...
GARRETT. Yeah probably. Word.
MARSHALL. But who fucking knows if she has a nice body 'cause it's like always covered up with all that ugly ass shit she wears.
GARRETT. *(laughing)* Word, yo...!

(snort-laughing)

Ugly ass shit....

(They laugh.)

(The unseen interrogator says something. They listen.)

(They stop laughing.)

(A beat. Then –)

MARSHALL.	GARRETT.
Oh. Yeah.	Oh. Yeah.

GARRETT. *(sheepishly)* Yeah.

MARSHALL. "*Had*" a nice body. I guess. Yeah.

(beat)

'Cause...

GARRETT. *(looking down; softly)* 'Cause she's dead.

MARSHALL. Yeah. So...yeah. So.

(Beat.)

MARSHALL.	GARRETT.
Shit.	Shit.

(**MARSHALL** *zips his hoodie up and down.* **GARRETT** *fidgets with his baseball cap.*)

(A beat. Then –)

(Blackout.)

SCENE 6.

(MIMI and AUGUST sit facing the audience. A bright light shines on their faces.)

(MIMI wears a tight-fitting black ensemble and files her nails with an emery board. AUGUST wears an expensive-looking suit and types on his Blackberry.)

MIMI. My daughter would *never* send a text like that.

AUGUST. My son wouldn't, either.

MIMI. She wasn't *raised* like that.

AUGUST. My son wasn't, either.

MIMI. She likes to have *fun*, sure.

AUGUST. My son does, too.

MIMI. They'll get into trouble sometimes, sure....

AUGUST. Tell me what teenager hasn't?

MIMI. But something that nasty???

AUGUST. I can't even imagine it.

(The unseen interrogator says something. They listen.)

(A beat. Then –)

AUGUST. *(re: his Blackberry)* Well, I'm *sorry*, but this is a very important –

MIMI. *(re: her emery board)* Well, I'm *sorry*, I didn't realize that this would be so dist*racting* –

MIMI.	**AUGUST.**
I can put it *away* if you want....	I can put it *away* if you want....

(They listen.)

(A beat. Then –)

(They begrudgingly put their props in their laps.)

MIMI. *(resentfully)* All right, you have my *full attention.*

AUGUST. All right, you have my full attention but I still don't see what –

MIMI. Yeah I still don't see why we're *here,* it's not like my daughter –

AUGUST. Yes it's not like my son –

(The unseen interrogator says something. They listen.)

(A beat. Then –)

MIMI. Well then there must be some mistake.

AUGUST. Yes, don't those things sometimes get –

MIMI. There must be some glitch...in the – technology...

AUGUST. Right, couldn't it have been – a con*fusion?* In the –

MIMI. I mean are you sure it was *her* number?

AUGUST. Are you sure it was *his* screen name?

(They listen.)

(A beat. Then –)

MIMI. Well then it must have been the other kids.

AUGUST. *(turning to Mimi)* What do you mean, "the other kids"???

MIMI. It must have been the other *kids.* In the – group...! Egging her on. Goading her! Pushing her to...do...! Such a thing....

AUGUST. *(indignant)* My son would never –

MIMI. *(turning to August)* I'm not saying *your son,* but I'm saying –

AUGUST. You *are* saying "*my son,*" you're saying –

MIMI. I'm *not* saying "your son," I don't know if your son is *capable* of such a / thing –

AUGUST. I *assure* you he is / *not!*

MIMI. – because he's so *high* out of his *mind* all the / time that –

AUGUST. Okay that's it. That's it. / That's it!

MIMI. "That's *it*"? *"That's it"*???

*(**AUGUST** stands and begins to walk out of the room.)*

(The unseen interrogator says something that stops him. He listens.)

(A beat. Then –)

AUGUST. Well, what do you want me to do? She's har*assing* me...!

MIMI. I am not *harassing* –

(The unseen interrogator says something. They listen.)

(A beat. Then –)

MIMI.	**AUGUST.**
Why aren't you dead already?	*Why aren't you dead already?*

(They process.)

(A beat. Then –)

MIMI. My daughter would *never* say something like that.

AUGUST. My son would absolutely *never* say *anything* even re*motely* like –

(The unseen interrogator says something. They listen.)

(A beat. Then –)

MIMI.	**AUGUST.**
Well then there must be some mistake.	Well then there must be some mistake.

(A beat. Then –)

*(**MIMI** picks up her emery board and resumes filing her nails.)*

*(**AUGUST** picks up his Blackberry and resumes typing away.)*

(A beat. Then –)

(Blackout.)

SCENE 7.

*(**CHRIS** sits facing the audience. A bright light shines on his face.)*

*(His vigor and swagger and high spirits are gone. His skin looks pallid, gray. His eyes look glazed over, vacant. He looks like a shell of the **CHRIS** we have seen.)*

(He plays with the sleeve of his sweatshirt – twisting it and rubbing it up and down his arm. He keeps his eyes down – on the floor.)

(He is quiet for a long, long time.)

(When he speaks, he speaks very softly. We have to strain to hear him.)

CHRIS. *(very softly)* ...yeah Idunno....

(A beat.)

(a little louder) Oh. Sorry. Yeah. I can be louder sorry.

(really loudly)

IDUNNO.

(beat; softer)

Sorry that was too loud. Sorry.

(A beat. He looks at his sleeve.)

Yeah I just. Idunno. I. Yeah. I loved her. Yeah.

(beat; looks at the ground)

...but like...

(beat)

...I couldn't *help* her, you know?

(beat)

...like... Idunno the right things to *say*... Idunno the right things to...

(trails off)

I wanted to *be* with her, but....

(beat)

...but like...someone had to be *saved*, you know...?

(beat)

...was I gonna go down too...?

(beat)

...sometimes you have to put your own oxygen mask on in order to....

(trails off; beat)

Idunno if that's true....

(beat)

But no one knows.

(beat)

I didn't tell anyone.

(beat)

Who would she have told?

(begins to cry)

...I was her only friend...!

(tries to stop crying)

I was her only friend.

SCENE 8.

(We stay in a blackout. We hear voices in the dark as the lights creep up slowly, slowly.)

MALLORY. No one really knew she had a *problem*....

TERESA. And like, everyone has *problems*, right?

LIZ. None of us thought it was this *serious*.

PETER. We didn't know. How could we *know*?

(Lights creep up, slowly, on the entire **ENSEMBLE**, *minus* **ANNA** *and* **CHRIS**, *facing the audience. A bright light shines on their faces.)*

MARSHALL. No one thought someone would really *do* something like that.

GARRETT. We were just having fun!

MIMI. If someone is suffering so much, they should *tell* someone....

AUGUST. If someone is in pain, they need to speak *up!*

(Somewhere else on stage, lights creep up slowly on **ANNA** *and* **CHRIS**, *in the cafeteria – the moment after she has grabbed his lacrosse stick. She holds on to it – her eyes locked into his. He holds on to the stick, too – his eyes locked into hers.)*

MALLORY. We can't read someone's *mind*.

TERESA. We can't know what you *mean*.

LIZ. I can't get in*side* my daughter....

PETER. I can't con*trol* my son....

MIMI. I don't have *time* for this drama...!

AUGUST. I don't know what else I can say.

(Tiny beat.)

ALL. I don't know what else I can say.

(Suddenly, **ANNA** *pulls on the lacrosse stick – strongly – pulling* **CHRIS** *toward her. He lets her, moves toward her.)*

(Their eyes stay locked on each other.)

(They are very close.)

(The electricity between them is palpable, penetrative – almost painful.)

(A beat. Then –)

(They kiss.)

(They kiss.)

(It is the sweetest, most innocent kiss in the world.)

(They kiss.)

(The ensemble keeps their eyes out, on the audience.)

*(**ANNA** and **CHRIS** kiss.)*

(They pull away, and look at each other.)

(The ensemble looks at us.)

(A beat. Then –)

(Blackout.)

(END OF PLAY)

www.ingramcontent.com/pod-product-compliance
Lightning Source LLC
Chambersburg PA
CBHW071411290426
44108CB00014B/1777